PROSTATE CANCER REVERSAL JUICING RECIPES COOKBOOK

31 QUICK AND EASY HOME-MADE NUTRIENT-RICH JUICE BLENDS TO HELP FIGHT PROSTATE CANCER AND PROMOTE HEALTH

Dr. Hellen S. McCoy

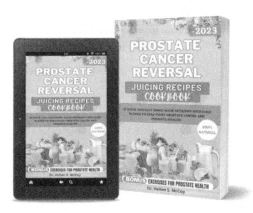

Dear Warrior on the Path to Healing,

In the face of adversity, you possess an unyielding strength that is nothing short of remarkable. As you navigate the challenging terrain of prostate cancer, remember that within you lies the power to shape your destiny.

This cookbook isn't just about recipes; it's a testament to your resilience. Each juice blend you create is a sip of hope, a toast to your courage, and a celebration of life's vibrant flavors. Through every measured pour and every revitalizing gulp, you're taking charge of your well-being.

In the world of uncertainty, these recipes are your allies – concoctions of nature's finest, designed to nourish your body and invigorate your spirit. As you blend, sip, and savor, visualize the nutrients working in harmony to strengthen your body's defenses and restore vitality.

Know this: you are not defined by your diagnosis, but by the grace with which you rise above it. You are an inspiration to those around you, a beacon of hope for others embarking on a similar journey. Your determination sends ripples of positivity far beyond the confines of your kitchen.

In times of doubt, remember the vibrant colors of the ingredients, the natural symphony of flavors, and the promise of rejuvenation in every glass. Embrace each day with the zest that comes from knowing that you're taking proactive steps towards your well-deserved health and happiness.

So, fellow traveler, raise your glass to resilience, to hope, and to a future where the chapters of triumph outnumber those of adversity. Let this cookbook be your constant reminder that you're not alone on this journey. Together, we juice, we heal, and we thrive.

With unwavering support and boundless hope,

[Dr. Hellen S. McCoy]

Hi

If you are a beginner, a vegan or a vegetarian, I am sure you will like to get the following books:

1. PLANT-BASED PROSTATE CANCER DIET COOKBOOK

Here is the link below:

https://My book to/PLANT-BASED-PROSTATE-CANCER-COOKBOOK

2. PROSTATE CANCER DIET COOKBOOK FOR MEN OVER 40

Here is the link below:

https://My book to/PROSTATE-CANCER-DIET-COOKBOOK

3. PLANT-BASED DIET COOKBOOK FOR CROH'NS AND COLITIS

Here is the link below:

https:///PLANT-BASED-COOKBOOK-CROHNS-COLITIS

4. PLANT-BASED DIET COKBOOK FOR KIDNEY HEALTH

Here is the link below:

My book to Plant based kidney health

5. PLANT-BASED CANCER DIET COOKBOOK

Here is the link below:

My book to Plant based cancer diet

6. ANTI-INFLAMMATORY JUICING COOKBOOK

Here is the link below:

My book to Anti-Inflammatory juicing recipes

7. And would you like to unlock delicious and nutrient- rich juice recipes to help you loose weight effectively and more ? Then I am sure you would like to get the following book:

INTERMITTENT FASTING SMOOTHIE AND JUICE RECIPES COOKBOOK

Here is the link below:

My book to effective weight loss

8. Likewise, would you like to enjoy delicious and easy to follow recipes to help you prevent and manage heart disease risk and support your heart health? Then I am sure you would like to get the following book:

HEART HEALTHY COOKBOOK FOR WOMEN OVER 50

Here is the link aside: My book to heart healthy recipes

TABLE OF CONTENTS

INTRODUCTION

In the journey of life, adversity often arrives uninvited, testing our resilience and determination. It's during these times that the human spirit truly shines, forging stories of triumph against all odds. Within the pages of **"Prostate Cancer Reversal Juicing Recipes Cookbook,"** we uncover a treasure trove of hope, health, and the remarkable journey of a man named David.

Imagine a life filled with zest and energy, the ability to conquer every challenge that comes your way. For David, this was once a reality. An avid outdoorsman, he reveled in the joy of hiking through rugged terrains, basking in the beauty of nature, and embracing life's adventures. But like an unexpected storm on a bright day, prostate cancer stormed into his life, threatening to dim his spirit and overshadow his dreams.

David's diagnosis was not just a medical verdict; it was a call to arms. He refused to let the formidable foe of cancer dictate the course of his life. With determination etched into every fiber of his being, he embarked on a quest for wellness, a quest that would lead him to the heart of holistic healing and the power of nutrition.

In the midst of uncertainty, David discovered the transformative potential of juicing, a symphony of flavors, colors, and nutrients that promised not only to strengthen his body but also to arm him with the tools to combat prostate cancer.

The idea was simple yet profound: harness the healing power of nature's bounty to nourish his body back to health.

And so, **"Prostate Cancer Reversal Juicing Recipes Cookbook"** was born. Within these pages, you will find more than just recipes; you will find a testament to the human spirit's tenacity and resilience. David's journey from despair to hope, from illness to wellness, is woven into each carefully curated blend. These juices are not mere concoctions; they are a lifeline, a lifeline that David used to pull himself back into the realm of vitality and vigor.

With 31 quick and easy home-made nutrient-rich juice blends, this cookbook is a guide to not only fighting prostate cancer but also promoting holistic health. From the zing of citrus to the comforting embrace of leafy greens, each recipe is a step toward rejuvenation. And as you sip on these vibrant elixirs, remember that you are sipping from the same cup of courage that David raised high in the face of adversity.

Dear friend, you hold in your hands more than a cookbook; you hold a promise. A promise that life's challenges can be conquered, that health can be reclaimed, and that every sip you take can be a step toward a brighter, healthier future. Let the story of David inspire you to take charge of your wellness journey. As you turn the pages and savor the flavors, may you find within these recipes the same hope that David found, the hope of reclaiming life's joys, one nutrient-rich blend at a time.

The role of juicing in prostate health

Juicing has gained popularity as a means to promote overall health and target specific health concerns, including prostate health. In the context of prostate cancer, juicing can play several roles that contribute to supporting prostate health and potentially aiding in the fight against prostate cancer.

Here are some key roles of juicing in prostate health:

Nutrient Delivery: Juicing allows for the consumption of a concentrated dose of vitamins, minerals, antioxidants, and phytochemicals from various fruits and vegetables. These nutrients are essential for supporting the immune system, reducing inflammation, and promoting overall well-being. For prostate health, specific nutrients like lycopene, vitamin C, vitamin E, selenium, and zinc are of particular importance.

Antioxidant Support: Many fruits and vegetables used in juicing are rich in antioxidants, which help neutralize harmful free radicals in the body. This is crucial because oxidative stress has been linked to various diseases, including prostate cancer. Antioxidants aid in the protection of cells and the maintenance of the body's natural defence systems.

Anti-Inflammatory Properties: Chronic inflammation is believed to play a role in the development and progression of various diseases, including prostate cancer. Certain fruits and vegetables, such as berries, leafy greens, turmeric, and ginger, have anti-inflammatory properties that can be beneficial for prostate health.

Lycopene Intake: Lycopene, a powerful antioxidant found in tomatoes and other red or pink fruits, has been specifically associated with prostate health. Studies suggest that lycopene may help reduce the risk of prostate cancer and slow its progression. Tomato-based juices can be a great source of lycopene.

Digestive Health: Juicing can provide a concentrated source of dietary fiber, which supports healthy digestion. A well-functioning digestive system ensures proper absorption of nutrients and elimination of waste products. This indirectly contributes to overall health and potentially prostate health.

Hydration: Adequate hydration is essential for maintaining overall health. Juices, especially those with high water content fruits like watermelon and cucumber, can contribute to hydration, which is important for cellular function and detoxification.

Weight Management: Maintaining a healthy weight is crucial for prostate health, as obesity has been linked to an increased risk of prostate cancer.

Juicing can be a part of a balanced diet that supports weight management by providing nutrient-rich options without excessive calories.

Alkalizing Effects: Some juicing ingredients, such as leafy greens and citrus fruits, have alkalizing effects on the body. An alkaline environment may help prevent the growth of cancer cells, as cancer cells tend to thrive in an acidic environment.

Supporting the Immune System: Juicing can provide a wide array of vitamins and minerals that are essential for a robust immune system. A strong immune system is crucial for the body's ability to recognize and fight off cancer cells.

Customization: Juicing recipes can be customized to include ingredients that are specifically beneficial for prostate health. This allows individuals to target their nutritional intake based on their unique needs and preferences.

It's important to note that while juicing can offer numerous health benefits, it should not be considered a sole treatment for prostate cancer or any other medical condition. Juicing can be a valuable addition to a balanced diet and a healthy lifestyle that supports overall well-being and prostate health.

Choosing the Right Ingredients

Maintaining a healthy diet is crucial for managing and preventing various health conditions, including prostate cancer. Juicing can be a great way to incorporate nutrient-rich ingredients into your diet to support prostate health.

Here's a comprehensive guide to choosing the right ingredients for juicing to promote prostate health:

Cruciferous Vegetables: Vegetables like broccoli, cauliflower, Brussels sprouts, kale, and cabbage belong to the cruciferous family. They contain compounds like sulforaphane that have shown potential in reducing the risk of prostate cancer. Include these vegetables in your juices to benefit from their anti-cancer properties.

Tomatoes: Tomatoes are high in lycopene, a potent antioxidant associated to a lower risk of prostate cancer. Lycopene is more easily absorbed when tomatoes are cooked or juiced, making tomato-based juices a great addition to your regimen.

Berries: Blueberries, strawberries, raspberries, and blackberries are packed with antioxidants and phytochemicals that can help combat inflammation and oxidative stress, contributing to prostate health.

Citrus Fruits: Oranges, grapefruits, lemons, and limes are high in vitamin C and other antioxidants, which play a role in protecting cells from damage. Vitamin C is essential for immune function and overall health.

Leafy Greens: Spinach, Swiss chard, and other leafy greens are rich in vitamins, minerals, and fiber. They provide a variety of nutrients that support overall health, including prostate health.

Pomegranate: Pomegranate juice is known for its high levels of antioxidants, particularly punicalagins and anthocyanins. These compounds have been linked to potential benefits in prostate health, including reducing inflammation and slowing the growth of prostate cancer cells.

Ginger and Turmeric: These spices contain anti-inflammatory compounds that can be beneficial for overall health and potentially for managing prostate issues.

Carrots: Carrots are a great source of beta-carotene, which is converted to vitamin A in the body. Vitamin A is essential for cell growth and immune function.

Green Tea: While not typically juiced, adding brewed and cooled green tea to your juices can provide additional antioxidants like catechins, which have been associated with various health benefits.

Nuts and Seeds: Flaxseeds, pumpkin seeds, and walnuts are rich in omega-3 fatty acids and other nutrients that may help support prostate health.

Watermelon: Watermelon contains citrulline, an amino acid that may have potential benefits for improving blood flow and promoting heart health, indirectly benefiting prostate health.

Garlic: Garlic contains compounds like allicin that possess anti-inflammatory and antioxidant properties. Including garlic in your juices can contribute to your overall health.

When creating your juicing recipes, aim for a balance of these ingredients to ensure you're getting a wide range of nutrients that support prostate health. Remember that while juicing can be a convenient way to consume these nutrients, it's important to also maintain a balanced diet that includes whole fruits, vegetables, lean proteins, and whole grains.

Tips for Efficient Juicing for Prostate Health

Here are some tips for efficient juicing to promote prostate health:

Fiber Consideration: Juicing removes much of the fiber present in whole fruits and vegetables. While this can be advantageous for easy digestion, remember that fiber also plays a role in maintaining gut health. You might want to complement your juicing routine with whole fruits and vegetables to ensure adequate fiber intake.

Organic and Fresh: Whenever possible, choose organic produce to reduce exposure to pesticides and other chemicals. Use fresh ingredients to maximize nutrient content.

Variety is Key: Rotate your ingredients to ensure a diverse range of nutrients. Different vegetables and fruits provide different health benefits, so changing up your recipes can be beneficial.

Hygiene and Cleanliness: Ensure your juicer and all utensils are thoroughly cleaned before and after each use to prevent the growth of harmful bacteria.

Portion Control: While juicing can provide a concentrated source of nutrients, it's important not to over consume.

Stick to reasonable portion sizes and consider juicing as a supplement to a balanced diet.

Remember that while juicing can offer nutritional benefits, it's essential to integrate it into a holistic approach to managing prostate health, including proper medical care, a balanced diet, regular exercise, stress management, and sufficient hydration.

Equipment and Ingredient Preparation

Here's a comprehensive guide:

Equipment:

Juicer: Invest in a good quality juicer. There are two main types: centrifugal juicers and masticating juicers. Centrifugal juicers are generally faster and easier to clean, but they might not extract as much juice from leafy greens. Masticating juicers work more slowly but are better at extracting nutrients from a wider range of produce.

Cutting Tools: You'll need a sharp knife and cutting board to prepare your ingredients before juicing. Ensuring your ingredients are appropriately sized will help with the juicing process.

Juice Containers: Have containers or bottles ready to collect and store the freshly made juice. Glass containers are preferable as they don't react with the juice and are easier to clean.

Strainer or Nut Milk Bag: Depending on the juicer you're using, you might need a fine strainer or nut milk bag to remove any remaining pulp from the juice if desired.

Cleaning Tools: A brush or tool designed for cleaning the juicer parts will be essential to keep your equipment in good condition.

Refrigerator or Cooler: Once you've juiced your ingredients, it's best to consume the juice immediately. If you need to store it, use an airtight container and keep it in the refrigerator for up to 24 hours.

Ingredient Preparation:

Organic Produce: Whenever possible, choose organic fruits and vegetables to reduce exposure to pesticides and chemicals.

Washing: Thoroughly wash all produce before juicing, even if you plan to remove the peel. This helps remove any dirt, bacteria, or residues.

Peeling: Some fruits and vegetables, like oranges and carrots, may need to be peeled before juicing. Others, like apples and cucumbers, can be juiced with the skin if they're organic and well-washed.

Cutting: Cut larger fruits and vegetables into smaller pieces that will fit easily into your juicer's feeding chute. This will help prevent clogs and ensure efficient juicing.

Variety: Aim for a variety of produce in your juice blends. This ensures a diverse array of nutrients and flavors. Include fruits and vegetables with antioxidants, vitamins, and minerals that support prostate health, such as tomatoes, broccoli, leafy greens, berries, and cruciferous vegetables.

Balance: While fruits can add natural sweetness and flavor to your juices, be mindful of their sugar content. Balance sweet fruits with low-sugar options like celery, cucumber, and leafy greens.

Portion Sizes: Keep in mind that juicing can concentrate calories and sugars, so moderate your portion sizes. A small glass of juice can provide a significant amount of nutrients.

Recipes: Consider trying various recipes that incorporate ingredients specifically known for supporting prostate health. For example, pomegranate, turmeric, green tea, and flaxseeds are often mentioned for their potential benefits.

31 HOME-MADE NUTRIENT-RICH JUICE BLENDS TO FIGHT PROSTATE CANCER

1. Green Vitality Elixir

Ingredients:

- 1 cup spinach leaves
- 1/2 cucumber
- 1 green apple
- 1/2 lemon (peeled)
- 1/2 inch ginger
- Water (as needed)

Method:

- Wash and prepare all ingredients.
- Cucumber and apple should be cut into small segments.
- Put all ingredients through a juicer.
- If required, add water to modify the consistency.
- Pour into a glass and enjoy!

Time: 10 minutes

Portion Size: 1 glass

2. Berry Burst Antioxidant Blend

Ingredients:

- One cup of mixed berries such as (blueberries, raspberries, and strawberries)
- 1/2 orange (peeled)
- 1/2 lemon (peeled)
- 1/2 cup watermelon chunks
- Water (as needed)

Method:

- Wash and prepare all berries.
- Cut the orange and lemon into small pieces.
- Juice the berries, orange, lemon, and watermelon.
- Add water to achieve the desired consistency.
- Pour into a glass and enjoy!

Time: 10 minutes

Portion Size: 1 glass

3. Citrus Immune Booster

Ingredients:

- 2 oranges (peeled)
- 1 grapefruit (peeled), 1 lemon (peeled)
- 1-inch turmeric root, Water (as needed)

Method:

- Wash and peel the citrus fruits.
- The turmeric root should be cut into tiny pieces.
- Juice the oranges, grapefruit, lemon, and turmeric.
- Add water to dilute if needed.
- Pour into a glass and enjoy!

Time: 10 minutes

Portion Size: 1 glass

4. Healing Ginger Carrot Fusion

Ingredients:

- 2 carrots
- 1 apple
- 1/2 lemon (peeled)
- 1-inch ginger
- Water (as needed)

Method:

- Wash and prepare the carrots and apple.
- Cut the apple into small pieces.
- Peel and slice the ginger.
- Juice the carrots, apple, lemon, and ginger.
- Adjust the consistency with water.
- Pour into a glass and enjoy!

Time: 10 minutes   **Portion Size:** 1 glass

5. Prostate Soothing Cucumber Refresher

Ingredients:

- 1/2 cucumber, 1 celery stalk
- 1 pear, 1/2 lemon (peeled)
- Handful of parsley, Water (as needed)

Method:

- Wash and cut the cucumber, celery, and pear.
- Chop the parsley leaves.
- Juice the cucumber, celery, pear, lemon, and parsley.
- Dilute with water if desired.
- Pour into a glass and enjoy!

Time: 10 minutes   **Portion Size:** 1 glass

6. Anti-Inflammatory Turmeric Twist

Ingredients:

- 1 apple, 1 orange (peeled)
- 1/2 lemon (peeled), 1-inch turmeric root
- 1/4 tsp black pepper, Water (as needed)

Method:

- Prepare the apple, orange, and lemon.
- Cut the apple into small pieces.
- Peel and chop the turmeric root.
- Juice the apple, orange, lemon, and turmeric.
- Add a pinch of black pepper.
- Adjust consistency with water.
- Pour into a glass and enjoy!

Time: 10 minutes   **Portion Size:** 1 glass

7. Cruciferous Powerhouse Mix

Ingredients:

- 1 cup kale leaves
- 1/2 cup broccoli florets
- 1/2 cup cauliflower florets
- 1 green apple
- 1/2 lemon (peeled), Water (as needed)

Method:

- Wash and prepare the kale, broccoli, and cauliflower.
- Cut the apple into small pieces.
- Juice the kale, broccoli, cauliflower, apple, and lemon.
- Adjust the consistency with water.
- Pour into a glass and enjoy!

Time: 10 minutes   **Portion Size:** 1 glass

8. Restorative Beetroot Blend

Ingredients:

- 1 small beetroot, 1 carrot
- 1 orange (peeled), 1/2 lemon (peeled)
- 1-inch ginger, Water (as needed)

Method:

- Wash and peel the beetroot, carrot, and orange.
- The beetroot and carrots should be cut into tiny pieces.
- Slice the ginger.
- Juice the beetroot, carrot, orange, lemon, and ginger.
- Adjust the consistency with water.
- Pour into a glass and enjoy!

Time: 10 minutes   **Portion Size:** 1 glass

9. Nutty Flaxseed Elixir for Hormonal Balance

Ingredients:

- 1 banana
- 1/2 cup strawberries,
- 1 tbsp flaxseeds
- 1/2 cup unsweetened almond milk
- Water (as needed)

Method:

- Wash and prepare the strawberries.
- The banana should be peeled and cut it into chunks.
- Blend the banana, strawberries, flaxseeds, and almond milk until smooth.
- If required, add water to modify the consistency.
- Pour into a glass and enjoy!

Time: 10 minutes   **Portion Size:** 1 glass

10. Healing Herbs and Greens Infusion

Ingredients:

- 1 cup spinach leaves, 1/2 cup parsley leaves
- 1/2 cup mint leaves, 1 cucumber
- 1/2 lemon (peeled), Water (as needed)

Method:

- Wash and prepare the spinach, parsley, mint, and cucumber.
- Cut the cucumber into small pieces.
- Juice the spinach, parsley, mint, cucumber, and lemon.
- Use water to adjust the consistency.
- Pour into a glass and enjoy!

Time: 10 minutes   **Portion Size:** 1 glass

11. Zesty Watermelon Detox

Ingredients:

- 2 cups watermelon chunks
- 1 lime (peeled)
- 1-inch ginger
- Handful of basil leaves, Water (as needed)

Method:

- Prepare the watermelon and lime.
- Peel and slice the ginger.
- Juice the watermelon, lime, and ginger.
- Chop the basil leaves.
- Add the chopped basil to the juice.
- Use water to adjust the consistency.
- Pour into a glass and enjoy!

Time: 10 minutes   **Portion Size:** 1 glass

12. Pineapple and Kale Anti-Cancer Blend

Ingredients:

- 1 cup pineapple chunks
- 1 cup kale leaves, 1/2 lemon (peeled)
- 1/2 inch turmeric root, Water (as needed)

Method:

- Wash and prepare the pineapple and kale.
- Cut the pineapple into chunks.
- Slice the turmeric root.
- Juice the pineapple, kale, lemon, and turmeric.
- Use water to adjust the consistency.
- Pour into a glass and enjoy!

Time: 10 minutes   **Portion Size:** 1 glass

13. Tomato Lycopene Elixir

Ingredients:

- 2 tomatoes
- 1 red bell pepper
- 1/2 cucumber
- 1/2 lemon (peeled)
- Handful of basil leaves
- Water (as needed)

Method:

- Wash and prepare the tomatoes, red bell pepper, and cucumber.
- Cut the cucumber into small pieces.
- Juice the tomatoes, red bell pepper, cucumber, and lemon.
- Chop the basil leaves.
- Add the chopped basil to the juice.
- Use water to adjust the consistency.
- Pour into a glass and enjoy!

Time: 10 minutes   **Portion Size:** 1 glass

14. Digestive Support Papaya Fusion

Ingredients:

- 1 cup papaya chunks
- 1/2 apple
- 1/2 lemon (peeled)
- 1/2 inch ginger
- Pinch of cinnamon
- Water (as needed)

Method:

- Wash and prepare the papaya and apple.
- Cut the apple into chunks.
- Peel and slice the ginger.
- Juice the papaya, apple, lemon, and ginger.
- Add a pinch of cinnamon to the juice.
- Use water to adjust the consistency.
- Pour into a glass and enjoy!

Time: 10 minutes

Portion Size: 1 glass

15. Energizing Maca and Berries Delight

Ingredients:

- One cup of mixed berries such as (blueberries, raspberries, strawberries)
- 1 banana
- 1 tbsp maca powder
- 1/2 cup coconut water
- Water (as needed)

Method:

- Wash and prepare the mixed berries.
- The banana should be and cut into small chunks.
- Blend the berries, banana, maca powder, and coconut water until smooth.
- Use water to adjust the consistency.
- Pour into a glass and enjoy!

Time: 10 minutes

Portion Size: 1 glass

16. Creamy Avocado and Spinach Nourishment

Ingredients:

- 1/2 avocado
- 1 cup spinach leaves
- 1/2 green apple
- 1/2 lemon (peeled)
- 1/4 cup unsweetened almond milk
- Water (as needed)

Method:

- Wash and prepare the spinach and apple.
- Cut the apple into small pieces.
- Blend the avocado, spinach, apple, lemon, and almond milk until creamy.
- Use water to adjust the consistency.
- Pour into a glass and enjoy!

Time: 10 minutes

Portion Size: 1 glass

17. Pumpkin Seed Protein Vitalizer

Ingredients:

- 1/4 cup pumpkin seeds, 1 banana
- 1/2 cup unsweetened almond milk
- 1/2 tsp cinnamon, Water (as needed)

Method:

- Blend the pumpkin seeds, banana, almond milk, and cinnamon until smooth.
- Use water to adjust the consistency.
- Pour into a glass and enjoy!

Time: 10 minutes   **Portion Size:** 1 glass

18. Radiant Skin and Prostate Health Elixir

Ingredients:

- 1 cup cantaloupe chunks, 1 carrot
- 1/2 orange (peeled), 1/2 lemon (peeled)
- Handful of mint leaves, Water (as needed)

Method:

- Wash and prepare the cantaloupe and carrot.
- Cut the carrot into small pieces.
- Juice the cantaloupe, carrot, orange, lemon, and mint.
- Use water to adjust the consistency.
- Pour into a glass and enjoy!

19. Kiwi Enzyme Boost for Immunity

Ingredients:

- 2 kiwis (peeled)
- 1/2 orange (peeled), 1/2 lemon (peeled)
- 1/2 inch ginger, Water (as needed)

Method:

- Wash and peel the kiwis, orange, and lemon.
- Slice the ginger.
- Juice the kiwis, orange, lemon, and ginger.
- Use water to adjust the consistency.
- Pour into a glass and enjoy!

Time: 10 minutes   **Portion Size:** 1 glass

20. Minty Celery Detox Refresher

Ingredients:

2 celery stalks, 1 cucumber

1/2 green apple, Handful of mint leaves

1/2 lemon (peeled), Water (as needed)

Method:

- Wash and prepare the celery, cucumber, and apple.
- The cucumber and apple should be cut into tiny pieces.
- Juice the celery, cucumber, apple, mint, and lemon.
- Use water to adjust the consistency.
- Pour into a glass and enjoy!

Time: 10 minutes   **Portion Size:** 1 glass

21. Alkalizing Cabbage and Apple Cleanse

Ingredients:

- 1 cup green cabbage, 1 green apple
- 1/2 lemon (peeled), 1/2 cucumber
- Handful of parsley, Water (as needed)

Method:

- Wash and prepare the cabbage, apple, cucumber, and parsley.
- The cucumber and apple should be cut into tiny pieces.
- Juice the cabbage, apple, lemon, cucumber, and parsley.
- Use water to adjust the consistency.
- Pour into a glass and enjoy!

Time: 10 minutes

Portion Size: 1 glass

22. Omega-3 Rich Flax and Blueberry Blend

Ingredients:

- 1/2 cup blueberries
- 1 banana
- 1 tbsp ground flaxseeds
- 1/2 cup unsweetened almond milk
- Water (as needed)

Method:

- Wash and prepare the blueberries.
- The banana should be cut into chunks.
- Blend the blueberries, banana, flaxseeds, and almond milk until smooth.
- Use water to adjust the consistency.
- Pour into a glass and enjoy!

Time: 10 minutes

Portion Size: 1 glass

23. Cranberry Antioxidant Kick

Ingredients:

- 1 cup cranberries
- 1/2 orange (peeled), 1/2 apple
- 1/2 lemon (peeled), Water (as needed)

Method:

- Wash and prepare the cranberries, orange, and apple.
- Cut the apple into tiny pieces.
- Juice the cranberries, orange, apple, and lemon.
- Use water to adjust the consistency.
- Pour into a glass and enjoy!

Time: 10 minutes   **Portion Size:** 1 glass

24. Healing Basil and Pineapple Elixir

Ingredients:

- 1 cup pineapple chunks
- 1/2 lemon (peeled)
- Handful of basil leaves
- 1/2 cucumber
- Water (as needed)

Method:

- Wash and prepare the pineapple and cucumber.
- Cut the cucumber into small pieces.
- Juice the pineapple, lemon, basil, and cucumber.
- Use water to adjust the consistency.
- Pour into a glass and enjoy!

Time: 10 minutes   **Portion Size:** 1 glass

25. Carotenoid-Rich Sweet Potato Elixir

Ingredients:

- 1 small sweet potato (cooked and cooled)
- 1 orange (peeled)
- 1/2 lemon (peeled)
- 1/2 inch ginger
- Water (as needed)

Method:

- Wash and prepare the cooked sweet potato.
- Peel and slice the ginger.
- Juice the sweet potato, orange, lemon, and ginger.
- Use water to adjust the consistency.
- Pour into a glass and enjoy!

Time: 10 minutes   **Portion Size:** 1 glass

26. Hormone Balancing Broccoli Blend

Ingredients:

- 1 cup broccoli florets
- 1/2 green apple, 1/2 lemon (peeled)
- 1/2 cucumber, Water (as needed)

Method:

- Wash and prepare the broccoli and apple.
- The apple and cucumber should be cut into tiny pieces.
- Juice the broccoli, apple, lemon, and cucumber.
- Use water to adjust the consistency.
- Pour into a glass and enjoy!

Time: 10 minutes   **Portion Size:** 1 glass

27. Red Grape Antioxidant Elixir

Ingredients:

- 1 cup red grapes
- 1/2 orange (peeled)
- 1/2 lemon (peeled)
- Handful of mint leaves
- Water (as needed)

Method:

- Wash and prepare the red grapes.
- Juice the red grapes, orange, lemon, and mint.
- Use water to adjust the consistency.
- Pour into a glass and enjoy!

Time: 10 minutes   **Portion Size:** 1 glass

28. Creamy Walnut and Banana Nourisher

Ingredients:

- 1 banana
- 1/4 cup walnuts
- 1/2 cup unsweetened almond milk
- 1/2 tsp vanilla extract
- Water (as needed)

Method:

- Blend the banana, walnuts, almond milk, and vanilla extract until smooth.
- Use water to adjust the consistency.
- Pour into a glass and enjoy!

Time: 10 minutes

Portion Size: 1 glass

29. Floral Hibiscus and Berries Elixir

Ingredients:

- 1/2 cup hibiscus tea (cooled)
- Half a cup of blueberries, raspberries, and strawberries)
- 1/2 orange (peeled), Water (as needed)

Method:

- Prepare hibiscus tea and let it cool.
- Wash and prepare the mixed berries.
- Juice the orange.
- Mix the hibiscus tea, berry juice, and orange juice.
- Use water to adjust the consistency.
- Pour into a glass and enjoy!

Time: 10 minutes

Portion Size: 1 glass

30. Nutrient-Dense Spinach and Mango Blend

Ingredients:

- 1 cup spinach leaves
- 1/2 mango (peeled and pitted), 1/2 lemon (peeled)
- 1/2 inch ginger, Water (as needed)

Method:

- Wash and prepare the spinach and mango.
- Cut the mango into chunks.
- Slice the ginger.
- Juice the spinach, mango, lemon, and ginger.
- Use water to adjust the consistency.
- Pour into a glass and enjoy!

Time: 10 minutes   **Portion Size:** 1 glass

31. Healing Turmeric and Orange Elixir

- **Ingredients:**
- 1 orange (peeled), 1/2 lemon (peeled)
- One teaspoon turmeric root, One teaspoon ginger
- Pinch of black pepper, Water (as needed)

Method:

- Wash and prepare the orange.
- Peel and slice the turmeric root and ginger.
- Juice the orange, lemon, turmeric, and ginger.
- Add a pinch of black pepper.
- Use water to adjust the consistency.
- Pour into a glass and enjoy!

Time: 10 minutes

Portion Size: 1 glass

Congratulations,

You now have the complete list of 31 Natural, low-sugar, low-salt, low-carb juice recipes that are perfect for healing Prostate cancer, diabetes, heart health, renal health, and overall well-being.

Enjoy these nutritious and flavorful juice blends!

BONUS

Effective and simple exercises for optimal prostate cancer health

Walking:

Step-by-Step Guide:

- ❖ Choose a serene and secure environment for your walk, like a local park, neighborhood, or even a treadmill.
- ❖ Commence your walk with a gentle warm-up, maintaining a slow and steady pace for approximately 5 minutes.
- ❖ Gradually escalate your speed to a brisk walk that allows you to converse but leaves you slightly breathless.
- ❖ Strive to engage in brisk walking for at least thirty minutes on most days of the week.
- ❖ As you conclude your brisk walk, transition into a leisurely stroll for another 5 minutes, followed by a sequence of tranquil stretches.

Cycling:

Step-by-Step Guide:

❖ Opt for a stationary bike or venture outdoors on a secure cycling route.
❖ Set the bike seat at a fitting height, ensuring a slight bend in your knees when the pedal is at its lowest point.
❖ Embark on your cycling journey at a moderate pace for a 5-minute warm-up.
❖ Amplify the intensity by pedaling faster or introducing resistance to mimic uphill cycling.
❖ Aim to cycle for duration of 20-30 minutes, encompassing three to five sessions each week.
❖ Conclude your cycling routine with a 5-minute gentle pedaling pace, followed by a series of rejuvenating stretches.

Resistance Training - Bodyweight Squats:

Step-by-Step Guide:

- ❖ Position your feet at shoulder-width distance, toes pointing outward.
- ❖ Begin by flexing your knees and pushing your hips back, emulating a seated posture.
- ❖ Uphold a tight core, maintain a straight back, and elevate your chest throughout the exercise.
- ❖ Lower yourself to a comfortable extent, striving to achieve parallel thighs with the ground.
- ❖ To return to the initial stance, exert pressure through your heels.
- ❖ Complete 2-3 sets of 10-15 repetitions for optimal results.

Resistance Training - Push-Ups:

Step-by-Step Guide:

- ❖ Commence in a plank position with hands slightly wider than shoulder-width apart, and feet together.
- ❖ Bend your elbows, ensuring your body forms a straight line, and gradually lower yourself towards the ground.
- ❖ Push back to the starting posture by fully extending your arms.
- ❖ If conventional push-ups prove challenging, modify by placing your knees on the ground.
- ❖ Execute 2-3 sets of 8-12 repetitions for a well-rounded workout.

Yoga - Child's Pose:

Step-by-Step Guide:

- ❖ Start in a tabletop position on your hands and knees.
- ❖ Sit back on your heels, extending your arms forward, and lowering your chest towards the ground.
- ❖ Rest your head on the floor or a yoga block.
- ❖ Take deep breaths and sustain the pose for 30 seconds to a minute.
- ❖ The Child's Pose promotes flexibility and relaxation by stretching the lower back, hips, and thighs.

Maintain a steady regimen to harness the full benefits of your exercise routine. If you encounter any discomfort or pain during your workout, cease immediately and consult a healthcare professional. Alongside these exercises, upholding a balanced diet, staying adequately hydrated, and adhering to your physician's guidance for prostate cancer management are pivotal for overall prostate health. Integrating a blend of cardiovascular exercises, resistance training, and yoga can significantly contribute to enhanced prostate cancer health and overall well-being.

CONCLUSION

As you close the pages of **"Prostate Cancer Reversal Juicing Recipes Cookbook,"** we hope you're armed with newfound knowledge and inspiration to embark on a journey towards enhanced prostate health. The journey you're about to undertake is not just about combating prostate cancer, but also about embracing a lifestyle that promotes overall well-being.

Throughout this cookbook, you've explored a collection of 31 quick and easy home-made juice blends meticulously designed to empower your body's defense mechanisms against prostate cancer. Each sip of these nutrient-rich elixirs is a step towards fortifying your body with the vitamins, minerals, and antioxidants it needs to thrive. But remember, this journey doesn't end here; it's a dynamic process that demands your commitment and dedication.

Incorporating these juicing recipes into your routine is not just about the physical act of preparing and consuming juices. It's about fostering a deep-rooted connection with your health and wellness. As you embark on this path to prostate health, consider it a holistic endeavor. Yes, the recipes provided within these pages offer a wonderful starting point, but they are merely the foundation upon which you can build a comprehensive lifestyle strategy.

It's important to remember that dietary choices are just one aspect of maintaining prostate health. Coupled with regular exercise, stress management, and consistent medical check-ups, these juicing recipes can become a formidable tool in your arsenal against prostate cancer. Furthermore, support from your healthcare provider and loved ones will be instrumental in navigating this journey effectively.

As you venture forth, keep in mind that progress is not always linear. There will be challenges, but your determination will be your greatest asset. Be patient with yourself, celebrate the small victories, and remain steadfast in your pursuit of prostate health.

In closing, this cookbook serves as more than just a compilation of recipes; it's a guide to taking control of your health and embracing a lifestyle that fosters longevity and vitality. May your journey be one of empowerment, healing, and renewed hope. Here's to your prostate health and the bright future that lies ahead.

Dear Reader,

Thank you for embarking on the journey to prostate health with our **"Prostate Cancer Reversal Juicing Recipes Cookbook."** We hope these nutrient-rich blends have inspired you to take charge of your well-being. Your dedication to your health is truly commendable.

We'd love to hear about your experience with the recipes and how they've impacted your journey. Your valuable insights could help us refine and enhance our offerings in the future. Feel free to share your thoughts through a simple review; it's all immensely valuable.

Remember, your commitment to a healthier lifestyle is a testament to your strength and resilience.

Cheers to your continued health and vitality!

Warm regards,

[Dr. Hellen S. McCoy]

Made in the USA
Las Vegas, NV
11 October 2024

96664222R00036